A GOOD STORY

Phil Parry

An extraordinary thirty five year award winning journalistic career in newspapers, television, radio and online as an incurable crippling disease struck.

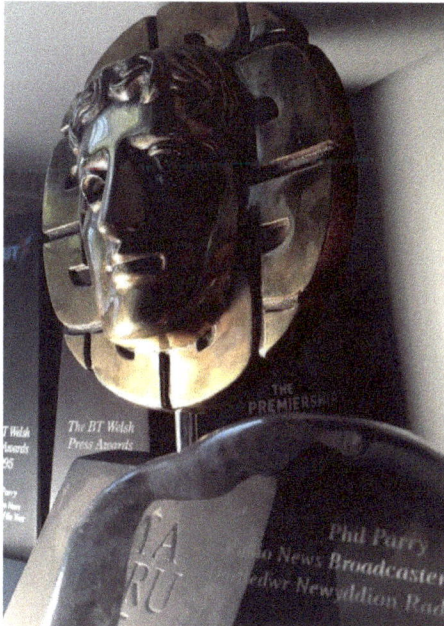

Phil won many awards for his journalism during his lengthy career.

Published by
Llyfrau Cambria Books, Wales, United Kingdom.
*Cambria Books is a division of
Cambria Publishing.*
Discover our other books at: www.cambriabooks.co.uk

CONTENTS

Introduction

These are the recollections of a long career in journalism during which I have been lucky enough to win several awards, as the incurable disabling condition *Hereditary Spastic Paraplegia (HSP)* was developing.

HSP is basically a corrosion of the nerves which makes walking a problem. I use a stick now and in a few years I will probably be confined to a wheelchair.

All these pieces have been published before on my website *The Eye,* so forgive the repetitions! It has struck me that I should pull them together and release them in a book. This is the result.

Boy scout.
Phil had always possessed a strong sense of duty!

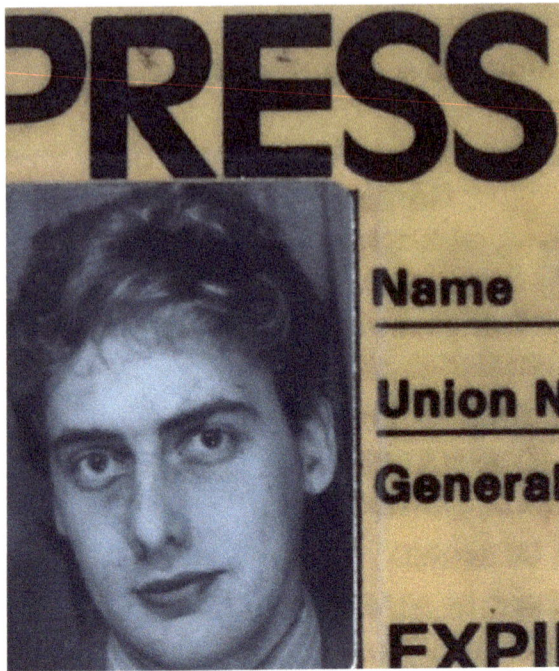

Press card.
A long career in journalism was ahead for Phil.

I started as a cub reporter on the *South Wales Echo* in August 1983 after coming out of *Manchester University* with a degree in *Politics and Modern History.*

Following a two-day 'induction' I was sent to Newcastle for several months to learn about basic reporting at the *Thomson Regional Newspapers (TRN)* training centre, doing stories for the *Evening Chronicle* and *The Journal.*

The Echo was then the biggest-selling paper produced in Wales, and the evening paper which covered Cardiff and the major South Wales valleys.

These things do not apply now.

In Newcastle we had to pass several exams in basic journalism such as in shorthand, law and public administration.

Back in Cardiff I signed for a two-year indenture period when you were legally bound to the paper and they had to train you.

You then saw a lot of people in very traumatic circumstances when you were still very young and heard extraordinary (often appalling) facts in court.

You were regularly sent to cover cases in *Magistrates Court* and *Crown Court.*

The training I received was excellent, and the TRN course at the time was reckoned to be second only to *The BBC's.*

I did stories in the main office, on the sub-editor's desk and in the district office of Bridgend, before sitting another load of exams.

You were trained in what does and does not constitute a story, the importance of accuracy and the legal rules which govern what can and cannot be published.

It seems a shame that this level of training is not apparently in fashion now.

There was little time for relaxing for Phil at Manchester University
He started a new student newspaper.

In the great age of the internet anyone can be a 'journalist' on social media, by 'publishing' 'information' or pictures, or by producing a blog.

Yet there has to be a role for a properly-trained journalist gate keeper who can say 'this is a good story' and 'that isn't a good story' or 'you are not legally allowed to say that'.

Legal rules are all-important.

Exactly the same laws apply on social media as on television or in newspapers, but people seem to be unaware of this.

The most appalling, often libelous, comments are made on social media for all to see.

During my time on the Echo I performed 'shifts' on several Fleet Street papers (all of the UK papers were located there or nearby but none are on 'the street' now) at weekends and during the holidays.

This was totally illegal of course, because you were bound to another paper, but it was seen as a way of getting on and everyone did them!

After the Echo I moved to a Cardiff freelance agency called *Cambrian News Agency* which made money by finding stories in the local patch which had a UK-wide interest and selling them on.

I got to know people on all the London-based papers, and the correspondents in South Wales and the South West.

The pay for journalists just starting out then was pretty miserable, and we lived on our expenses or 'exes'.

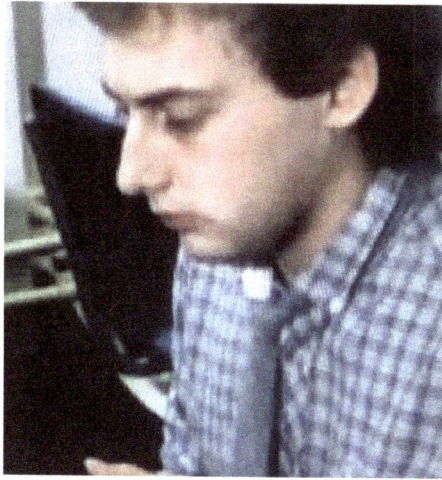

Phil on Echo as a young reporter.
When still a very young reporter Phil often had to interview people
in traumatic circumstances. © *BBC*

At the Echo you were allowed a 'set' level of expenses to 'claim' even if you never left the office - again totally illegal because it was undeclared income.

I joined the Echo on less than £5,000 a year and at Cambrian my pay went up to the princely annual sum of £6,000.

During my time at Cambrian I was 'hired out' to *HTV Wales* (it's now *ITV Wales*).

This gave me experience in television so I could 'sell' myself and after reporting for the evening news on *Wales at Six* at HTV, I went to the BBC where I stayed for 23 years, first on *Wales Today* then the TV Current Affairs programme *Week In, Week Out* (WIWO) which has been axed after 53 years.

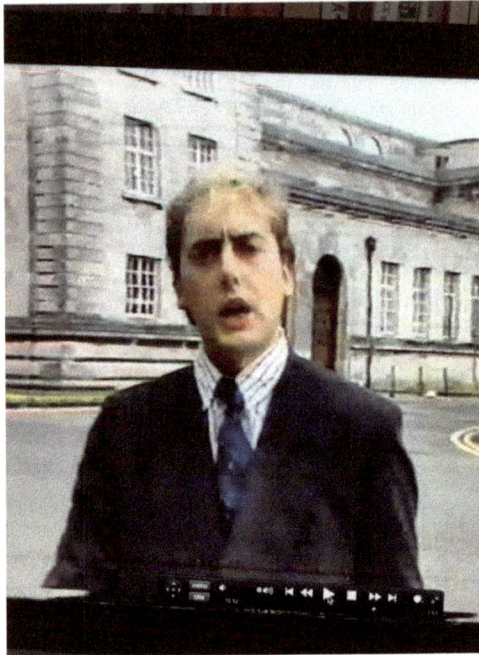

Phil began his 23 year career at the BBC on 'Wales Today'

Phil at WIWO ©BBC

It is a great pity that regular Current Affairs television is not in favour now and seen as costly.

So many of them have gone apart from WIWO.

On the BBC those that have closed include *Public Eye* and *Rough Justice*, while on ITV the cull has been even worse and *World in Action, TV Eye, This Week* and *First Tuesday* have all shut their doors.

Staying in television, I transferred to London and worked as a reporter on *Public Eye, Newsnight* and *Panorama*.

But I wanted experience in live broadcasting, so I moved in to radio and at *BBC Radio Wales* I presented any number of live daily or weekly programmes.

On these broadcasts I could hone my tough interviewing style after earning a reputation for putting hard-ball questions in set-piece TV interviews.

A lot of people became very angry with me, and on one occasion a *Panorama* I was fronting was such a sensitive programme that a security expert was called in to check my movements and my family home was wired for intruders with panic-buttons in the hall and at my bedside.

One highly experienced former BBC colleague and friend said I was the bravest journalist he had ever known.

What I do now

After I left the BBC I started tripping and was finally diagnosed with the incurable condition HSP.

As my consultant explained it this is basically a corrosion of the nerves to your legs, and as the name implies you have it from birth, but it becomes gradually worse as you get older.

I could not do any of the things that I did as a young man and now work on *The Eye* from home.

Phil now works from home on the Eye Magazine

But as long as I have a telephone, notebook and pen I can still cause trouble!

It's all here. Enjoy!

Phil Parry – January 2019

Yet another good story. Pt.1

I even have a vivid memory of the squeak of the newsroom door on my first day.

The room was open plan, and at the time, *The South Wales Echo,* where I started as a cub reporter, shared it with *The Western Mail* across a stained carpet.

The 'tea station' was in the middle, along with the 'typewriter graveyard', which consisted of several desks pushed together with machines waiting to be fixed, piled on top.

It was always comforting when the print machines (which were below then) were running.

It meant your story would soon be out on the streets in Cardiff.

On the way to the newsroom you passed a 'viewing gallery' where you could look down on the print room and see your copy coming off the presses – it was always an exciting moment.

Over the years I have withstood any number of spurious legal threats and a thorough knowledge of the libel laws is essential in journalism – a lesson I was first taught after passing my initial *National Council for Training Journalists (NCTJ)* exams.

Looking back, I realise I was exposed to moments of terrible drama when I was still very young, including being a first-hand witness to the violence on picket lines during the '84 –

'85 miners' strike.

I often think the 80s and 90s were a fine time to be a young reporter in South Wales because so much happened. Apart from the miners' strike, there was mass unemployment after huge structural change in the economy, all the deep pits were closed down (which I never thought would happen) and voters narrowly voted for devolution following a closely-fought referendum campaign.

I presented a *Newsnight* film during that campaign, trying to explain the issues to a UK audience.

One tragic story I remember well, developed in the Ely area of Cardiff after a young mother had nipped out to buy cigarettes leaving her two small children alone – they found matches and burnt the house down, dying in the process.

I was despatched by my News Editor Stuart 'Minto' Minton to secure an interview with the grieving mother and I arrived to find her picking through the ruins of her house.

Apart from the training I received to pass exams, in those days another crucial aspect of journalism was to retrieve a picture for the 'story' – the so-called 'pick-up pic' (this was of course long before Social Media!). So I asked this poor woman for a picture of her two small children who had died, and she bent down to pull a picture out of the burnt carpet. It had scorch marks around the edges.

After she had given me a very tearful interview, I drove her to a nearby social security office so that she could claim special benefits.

I was only twenty two.

To make this awful tragedy even worse, I was told we could not actually use the picture she had given me, because it was one of those special sepia-toned ones, where the children were all dressed up as though they were in the wild west, and it would have looked ridiculous with a story like this.

From the Echo I moved to a freelance agency on *Charles*

Street in *Cardiff* called *Cambrian News Agency* when I was still only 23, where you made money by getting stories in South Wales and 'flogging' them to the UK papers. You always had to look for an angle to the story so that it might appeal to Mrs Jones in Carlisle.

I had left the Echo before the end of my training 'indentures' period, and the Editor, Geoff Rich, said I would never work there again.

A witty friend of mine said I should have asked for that in writing!

We covered a lot of court cases on Cambrian and a story that sticks in my mind was about a lesbian couple who had had a fierce row, during which one of them left. She then got her gay friends in London to come to Cardiff and firebomb her former partner's house (again in Ely). They were all up at *Cardiff Crown Court* on various charges (a multi-hander as it was known) and the evidence was unequivocal, so they were found guilty.

During my time at the agency, and before on the Echo, I did shifts with other news organisations such as the *Daily Mail* (where a certain Paul Dacre was then News Editor) and *Today* newspaper.

At Cambrian I was 'hired' out to do shifts at *HTV Wales,* as it then was before it became *ITV Cymru Wales,* and this experience secured me a job at *BBC Wales* which is where I was for 23 years.

The great thing about the BBC is that it is so large you can move around. I took full advantage and worked on BBC 2's *Public Eye* as well as *Newsnight* and *Panorama* on *BBC One.*

In TV news I worked on *Wales at Six* on *HTV Wales,* and *Wales Today* on *BBC Wales.* I also presented countless programmes for *BBC Radio Wales.*

But the role I suppose I am best known for at *BBC Wales,*

was presenting the weekly TV Current Affairs series *Week In, Week Out* which is sadly no more, and I was lucky enough to win numerous awards while I was there.

In my early days in television, I was very concerned with how I looked on screen and after my first 'piece-to-camera' I asked a friend: "Were my eyes looking at the camera".

He replied: "Well, one of them was".

I THINK he was joking...

After the BBC I became the founding Editor of *The Eye* and we have broken numerous stories.

When I told a reporter friend of mine that I had been a journalist for 35 years, he said: "I bet you can remember your first story" and he was absolutely right – I could!

My first story was about badger-baiting in South Wales, and my second story was about a huge dog which had been taken in by the RSPCA.

'Minto' inquired when I gave him my copy: "How much does the dog eat?". This was an excellent question, but I hadn't actually asked it!

So, a story about a dog taught me a lesson I carried with me through the rest of my career. Always ask the right question!

In 35 years I have covered thousands of stories.

But those first ones were all-important...

Yet another good story. Pt.2

After a 23 year stint with the BBC during which I presented, among other programmes, the now-defunct TV Current Affairs series *Week In, Week Out (WIWO)* on *BBC Wales, BBC One's Panorama* and *Newsnight* films, as well as *Public Eye* on *BBC 2*, I took charge of the investigative news website *The Eye*.

It seems a shame to me that WIWO is no more.

The series, and I, had won numerous awards – among them *BAFTA Cymru, The Royal Television Society [RTS], BT Wales Best Journalist of the Year* and at the *Celtic Media* ceremony.

An edition of WIWO called 'A *Night To Remember'* secured new information which led to the release from prison of three young South Wales men, after they had spent 11 years in jail following a wrongful conviction for murder. I had been privileged to experience any number of amazing things at the BBC, and throughout I had never been afraid to ask people in positions of influence difficult questions which invariably attracted complaints.

I have knocked on the front doors of dodgy business people and crooked police officers, and I had learned to take a step back in case they came out swinging when they answered the door.

I am glad to say they usually went for the camera next to me!

When I worked on a *Panorama* programme which was effectively accusing someone of murder, a security expert was

15

sent from London to check my movements.

An intruder-alarm was installed at my house which had panic buttons in the hall and at my bedside.

One highly-experienced former colleague and senior executive at the BBC kindly said I was the bravest journalist he had ever known.

It became clear, though, that my style of journalism was going out of fashion, as I prompted too many complaints for the liking of senior management.

Some of the targets were, after all, friends of those in charge of me!

So I had to become the founding Editor of *The Eye* to conduct the kind of journalism I believed in.

In a short existence our journalists have disclosed a series of important stories, many of which were taken up by the UK media, although not by the mainstream Welsh media and we are continuing to do so today.

I have personally withstood numerous legal threats and suffered huge abuse on social media.

This is part of one of the social media attacks on me and *The Eye* from a crook we have exposed: "I am have contacted you (sic) numerous times before asking why you consistently, stalk, bully and harass (sic) me? ... You so far have asked the following for comments
Thief
Abuser *(The Eye have never said this person is an abuser)*.
Liar
Sex Offender *(The Eye have never said this person is a sex offender)*.
Drug user *(The Eye have never said this person is a drug-user, just that he has dealt in illegal drugs)*.

His wife has also bombarded *The Eye* and me, with insulting messages on social media.

Among them was this response to a picture of me: "The face

of a real life bully... don't you look so proud tooawww".

I have been called, wrongly, "biased" and "misogynistic" on *Twitter* as well as a "lying bastard" and "vermin" on the internet.

These are very serious charges to make of a journalist.

If you become known as these things then you are not viewed as independent, and it rules out doing the job.

People seem to be unaware that all the same legal rules apply to comments on social media, as with a page lead in a newspaper or an item on *Wales Today*.

Yet the most appalling things are said on *Facebook* and *Twitter*.

I spent many hours in classrooms to pass exams in journalist law, because knowledge of libel is essential in my business.

In the world of politics we have questioned the decision by Labour's Welsh *First Minister* (FM) at the time, Carwyn Jones to answer *First Minister's Questions* (FMQs) rather than attend the Memorial Service in Manchester cathedral to those who had died in the terrorist outrage in the city.

We have also published a piece drawing attention to the inconsistencies of a Labour *Assembly Member's (AM)* call for rent controls (popular in Cuba), when a huge number of non-EU students rent homes in Cardiff and boost the Gross Domestic Product (GDP) of the area.

It had emerged this AM had also faced enormous criticism for advertising to employ a gardener at public expense.

The Eye hold no political allegiance, although we have been accused, incorrectly, of being part of the Labour party.

There appears to be an unwillingness in parts of the mainstream Welsh media to take on influential people, and to conduct long-term investigations. These are important and need to continue – perhaps now more than ever, despite the complaints you receive when you undertake them.

As now with our pieces on *The Eye*, in all the TV programmes I have presented, every word would be double-checked by libel lawyers; yet despite this people would usually complain about things that were NEVER said.

In the miscarriage of justice investigations, I have pursued over the years it always struck me as odd that a pervasive attitude (especially among a murder victim's family) was for ANYONE to be convicted – never mind if it was the wrong person.

Apart from the demise of WIWO on *BBC Wales TV* as well as a host of other TV Current Affairs series on network television, 'clickbait' journalism, and writing lists, appears to prevail, despite denials.

Sexist 'stories' about beauty contests in Wales are 'reported', along with the opening of bars which feature scantily-clad women dancing for a largely-male clientele.

I was horrified when it was suggested by the Editor of a website in Wales, to someone anxious to break into journalism, that writing lists about the best street food was the way to do it.

The Editor of the website wrote: "You might not be interested in 19 mouth watering street food dishes and where to find them in Wales, and you might believe it's not something we should be writing (I wouldn't agree, but that's fine).

"That doesn't mean it's clickbait."

This is NOT the kind of journalism I recognise.

It is a pity that the kind of investigations I do is not in favour now, because there is so much emphasis on chasing ratings in broadcasting, along with making money in the independent sector and on newspapers.

Investigations, such as those on *The Eye,* are not cost-effective.

They take a lot of work, and often many months to complete – therefore they do not lend themselves easily to accounting in journalism.

The stories do not fit into boxes.

Sometimes we can work on something for a long time and it can cost a great deal of money, yet it might come to nothing.

These investigations are, though, vital and hold important people to account.

Fight Club

When you are young you lead a fairly sheltered life.

I was certainly shaken out of this happy existence when I joined the *South Wales Echo* as a trainee reporter at the tender age of 21 in 1983.

On one famous occasion I watched through the corner of my eye as the *News Editor* of the paper, Stuart Minton, thumped a reporter because he was swearing at him in front of his daughter.

His victim fell at my feet as I sat perched on one of the desks talking to a friend.

This extraordinary incident happened because Stuart had not signed the reporter's expenses, which he relied on, and he would be left without money for the weekend.

Screams echoed around the newsroom as people realised what had just happened.

For somebody fresh out of university, when you are used to people being nice to each other, this was eye-opening.

The other part of 'getting your knees brown' as Stuart used to say, was identifying the long list of characters in the Echo newsroom.

One produced excellent copy in the morning, but his accuracy couldn't be relied on in the afternoon because he'd had a few drinks.

Another reporter saw him talking to me and mimed lifting

a glass to his mouth behind his back.

A shambolic figure who was widely-liked in the newsroom, told me he had left his previous paper because he didn't like the way the *News Editor* hung up his coat!

This reporter had supposedly fallen asleep in a chair with a meat pie in his pocket, woke up, found the pie and carried on eating it.

Another reporter covered Cardiff's magistrates court in the morning but in the afternoon (because there was rarely a case to cover) he spent the time squirrelled away in the city's central library looking at back copies of the paper and preparing 'Echoes of the Echo'.

He was known as 'mad Jack' and was allegedly blown over by a freak gust of wind when we were reporting news of a gale which had struck South Wales.

A feature writer on the sister newspaper *The Western Mail* in the same newsroom who I knew well, we were told, had actually fallen asleep DURING an interview with one of his subjects because he was so boring!

You know the kind of thing: "I stormed ashore during the war..."

"ZZZZZ."

One reporter who covered a lot of crime stories was a fairly tall character and wore a long dark coat.

He told me how he was often mistaken for a police officer on the doorstep.

He never lied or did it deliberately (which would have been against the law) but he was aware of the mix-up and didn't disabuse his interviewee because he could get more information that way.

21

Seeing extraordinary characters and watching fights in the newsroom - they were swift wake up calls alerting a young reporter to how life really was in journalism!

Scrooge

For trainee reporters on local newspapers there are real hardships.

You cannot afford any luxuries beyond a few pints, and you always have to count the pennies when it comes to living accommodation.

Anyway, that was certainly the case when I started on the *South Wales Echo* 35 years ago.

It has only just struck me how long ago this was and the shock is palpable!

Over Christmas 1983 I looked round a rented 'flat' on Clive Street in the Grangetown area of Cardiff with a mate of mine who was the trainee reporter on the *Western Mail* called Tim.

We decided to take it – on conditions.

This flat was on the third floor of a house, and every room had its own meter, with the rooms giving out onto a tiny rubbishy kitchen which had only a skylight for illumination.

All the rooms were under the eaves and the roof leaked so there were enormous bulges in the wallpaper where the water collected.

One of the bulges was just above my head in the bed and I was always worried it might burst in the night!

On the floor below us there was an Iraqi while on the ground floor there was an Iranian – this was at the height of the Iran/Iraq war and the pair used to have enormous arguments.

23

There was only a single shower and toilet for the entire house (no bath as I remember, although there must have been one somewhere) and dark hairs used to collect on the grill for the shower's waste pipe.

Apart from the two bedrooms for Tim and me, there was a small box room without a window – it had only a skylight, and this too had its own meter. As we were being shown round the flat by the landlord, it dawned on me that he was going to rent out this box room separately, so we negotiated to rent that room too.

Our rent went up to the princely sum of £11 a week....

Taking the Biscuit

A huge part of a journalist's training was signing for the two year 'indentures' period with your local paper or media group.

These were usually very formal affairs involving the Editor, News Editor, and Managing Director (MD), where they would go so far as to provide such luxuries as biscuits!

The indentures papers I signed were in the office of the MD of the *Western Mail and Echo,* Howard Green.

He was in charge when I started officially as a cub reporter on the *South Wales Echo* – then the biggest-selling newspaper produced in Wales.

He was the father of the former First Secretary of State, Damian Green, who was sacked from the UK cabinet over being "inaccurate and misleading" about what he knew concerning pornography on his office computer in 2008.

So I knew Howard Green a little – and note with sadness that he has died.

He was a journalist of the old school who believed it was very important to train young reporters in subjects such as law, public administration and how actually to TALK to people!

The latter sounds absurd but is probably the most important thing of all.

In a very short time over the phone or on the doorstep, you need to come over as friendly, genuine and trustworthy to someone who is, perhaps, in the middle of the most traumatic experience he or she will ever face.

There is a way of phrasing questions so they are not too intrusive, yet secure the information you need.

All of this was well known to Mr Green, who was MD of my newspaper company in the *Thomson Regional Newspapers* (TRN) group from 1981 to 1985.

He was launch Editor of the *Evening Post* in Reading (also in the TRN group) and took its circulation to 55,000 in just four years – figures about which Editors of Welsh newspapers now can only dream!

Before signing the indentures in Mr Green's office, I was told what to expect by my News Editor Stuart 'Minto' Minton (also now sadly-departed).

In a magnificent wind up, one poor fellow trainee reporter had been persuaded he would have to sing the company song!

We even wrote it out for him to learn.

One of the lines was: "From shore to shore the pen is mightier than the sword".

I remember that during the signing process I managed to demolish all the biscuits.

Mr Green never forgot it – and kept reminding the Editor of the Echo, Geoff Rich.

From then on, we reported a daily round of stories about damp council flats or chip pan fires; during three months in head office in Cardiff, three months in a district office and three months on the subs desk, then back to Cardiff where we completed our training.

But there were no more biscuits.

Unfortunately!

Good Circulation

The plunging newspaper circulation may not matter to some senior executives.

When I started as a cub reporter on the Cardiff-based *South Wales Echo* in 1983 it was the biggest-selling newspaper produced in Wales and had a circulation of more than 80,000.

Today the circulation is a fraction of that and the Echo has long-since been overtaken – first by the *South Wales Evening Post* based in Swansea, and then by the regional morning paper which serves North Wales, *The Daily Post*.

The circulation of most UK newspapers has also fallen dramatically over the same period.

To take as an example, *The Guardian*, which has recently relaunched with a new properly-tabloid size after a lengthy period with the ridiculous 'Berliner' format, sold at one point less than 148,000 a day.

The Times was pleased to have sold 446,204 copies in one month.

Yet these apparently gloomy statistics may not matter.

Cutting costs (for which read getting rid of people) could be more important.

For instance, *The Guardian* has 'cut costs', slashed losses, and is starting to turn a corner.

Today the publisher has a new reader-revenue driven business model and is on the brink of breaking even.

The paper has halved its operating losses.

In the usual business-speak, *Guardian Media Group* (GMG) Chief Executive Officer at the time David Pemsel. said: "The media sector remains challenging.

"However, our reader revenues are growing well, our advertising proposition remains strong, and more people are reading us than ever before."

So, profits matter today almost more than circulation figures.

But the number of people who are prepared to pay to read news in newspapers is still worryingly low, and in Wales the picture is especially disturbing.

It has been reported that *The Daily Post* was Wales' best-selling regional newspaper, and the print sector remains in long-term decline.

Figures for 2016 showed that the paper sold an average of 22,251 copies.

But even that was a fall from the 23,645 printed copies sold in 2015.

The Post's circulation had overtaken the *South Wales Evening Post,* which had an average circulation in 2016 of 21,031 copies.

The *Western Mail,* which styles itself as 'the national newspaper of Wales', saw its circulation fall to 15,697 copies in 2016, down from an average of 18,063 the previous year.

There was an average circulation in the late 2010s of around 10,800 for the Newport-based *South Wales Argus,*

Wales on Sunday (WoS) has also lost readers, reaching an average circulation of 11,608 in 2016 compared to 14,314 the previous year.

The hit rate for the *Media Wales'* website version *WalesOnline* is far greater and this was thought to provide the supposed digital future.

But knowledge of the libel laws can be sketchy and we were threatened with court action after an accurate satirical piece. The extraordinary words were used 'satire is no defense against libel' when in fact it can be. A reader of the website in question who was anxious to break into journalism was advised by the Editor: "You might not be interested in 19 mouth watering street food dishes and where to find them in Wales, and you might believe it's not something we should be writing (I wouldn't agree, but that's fine)."

"That doesn't mean it's clickbait."

But this kind of journalism is not popular among the staff there.

As one reporter told us: "All we seem to do is lists about the best places to have a cup of coffee in Wales, and the only things we can be sure will get in are 'stories' about celebs, rugby or the weather".

The opening of bars has also proved fruitful territory for some websites. 17 stories were published about one in Cardiff in 2016. A reader said sarcastically about the 'reports' "Scantily clad women dancing on a bar, serving drinks in-between, whilst men look on but can't touch? No sexism there. At all."

Another said: "I think someone needs to look up what sexism is, because this is exactly that."

The owner of 'Media Wales', which includes the website 'WalesOnline' as well as the newspapers 'South Wales Echo', 'WoS' and 'The Western Mail', 'Trinity Mirror' brought in a 'Digital First' strategy as part of the 'Connected Newsroom' scheme when 'target hit rates' were introduced, to try and counter the trend of falling circulation and embrace the supposed digital future.

But as we reported some digital companies are facing severe

challenges and maybe old-fashioned journalism is on the way back.

Now there's a thought...

Accident Waiting to Happen

Along with crime stories, car crashes are a mainstay of local journalism.

But the reporter is not normally the focus of the crash.

Yet it happened to me when I was in the 'Echo pool car' as a cub reporter in 1984.

I was returning from an interview in a Cardiff suburb, and I knew a good story was in my notebook, so I only had to write it up in the office.

I was singing along to the radio coming down a hill, and driving far too fast, when I lost control of the car and crashed it.

I didn't hit anyone, and nobody (including myself) was hurt, but I had hit a high kerb and bent the subframe of the car.

It was a write-off.

Another Echo reporter was sent out to come and pick me up.

The car was taken back to the *Western Mail and Echo* garage, where they decided it could not be fixed and we would have to get a new one.

But there is an addendum to this story.

Luckily it was also spotted that a tyre was almost bald, although it had nothing to do with the accident, and it seemed a miracle to them that I had got out unharmed.

I became the hero of the hour, rather than the villain and

another – safer – car appeared for reporters.

Only now am I revealing that the cause of the accident was actually ME, not the bald tyre!

It is another exclusive scoop.

But for someone else this time!

A Tough Act

In journalism it is always important to 'get on'.

It certainly was when I started as a cub reporter on *The South Wales Echo* in 1983.

You were constantly looking for your next move up the ladder into broadcasting or on to the 'nationals' (UK) newspapers.

The way to do this was to do 'shifts' at the papers in London during the weekends and over holidays, which got your face known at newspapers there.

It was all completely illegal of course, because you were contracted to another paper (obviously the Echo knew all about it but the bosses turned a blind eye).

My old News Editor on the Echo, Stuart Minton, always used to send me on difficult stories with the words "you should get your knees brown", which I thought was an odd expression, although I knew what he meant.

The following experience, though, was even more useful – even more important than having a thorough knowledge of the law and covering court cases.

It taught me the importance of 'toughening up' as a reporter because you see some pretty awful sights, and you are called pretty terrible names!

In early 1987 I did shifts on *The Daily Mail* where the News Editor was a certain Paul Dacre, who went on to become Editor of the Mail and Editor-in-Chief of the publisher of the paper, which includes *The Mail on Sunday,* the free tabloid *The Metro,* the *Mailonline* website, as well as other titles.

It was the days when 'creative tension' was very much in vogue, and you could cut like a knife the atmosphere in the Mail newroom

Paul Dacre was actually OK to me, although he had a fearsome reputation, but his deputy was AWFUL, and for an extremely green young reporter he was a frightening sight.

For one story I had to write a 'tribute' to a Hollywood star who had just died.

To do this, I had to contact the dead star's agent.

I had no idea how to get hold of the contact details and had to ask someone in another department.

I also had no idea how actually to file the piece.

The result was that it took several hours before I wrote the copy and put it in the system.

When the Deputy News Editor saw it he grabbed it (these were the days when it was a physical version) and stalked down the newsroom to my desk.

"I THOUGHT YOU SAID YOU WERE QUICK!" he shouted at me.

I didn't know what to say in reply and stammered something back.

He marched back to his desk in a foul mood.

For a young and innocent 23-year-old, fresh out of university, who was used to seeing people be nice to each other as he was growing up, this was pretty shocking stuff.

I had now witnessed real anger, and even a fight over expenses in the Echo newsroom!

But I am always keen to put a positive gloss on things, and these are extremely useful experiences – so I am grateful!

Pedal Power

For newspapers promotions have always been important.

A central one for *The South Wales Echo,* which I covered in 1984, was the *On Your Bike for Barnardo's* cycle ride.

This was a gruelling 38-mile charity bicycle ride around the Vale of Glamorgan and is still run today.

A newspaper's circulation and marketing departments are constantly working together to come up with promotional ideas to increase sales or link up with events like this one in their area.

Today, with newspaper circulations under pressure as never before, this kind of scheme is needed more than ever.

You were awarded a fairly cheap 'medal' if you completed the *'On Your Bike'* ordeal, and I coined the rather cheesy phrase "**Pedal For A Medal**" which you will still see used in the paper today.

I was expected to provide regular copy for the newspaper on the weird and wonderful entrants to drum up support for the bike ride and push up sales.

Luckily there was a ready supply of stories, such as the first entrant, the regular entrant, the fancy dress entrant, and so on.

I also had to take part in the event myself (this was long before my Hereditary Spastic Paraplegia (HSP) took hold – I couldn't do it now) which was another experience altogether.

We set off from *Sophia Gardens* in Cardiff, and the start

was heralded by my now-departed Editor Geoff Rich waving a flag.

In fairness to Geoff Rich (who was not universally liked), I remember he spotted me and shouted: "Good luck Phil!" as I passed.

Within a few miles I was worn out (I had done no training whatsoever).

The photographer for the Echo spotted me pushing my bike up a hill just outside Cardiff, and he predictably got out of the car and took a picture of me which was duly used in the paper!

The headline was "**Our Exhausted Reporter Pushes His Bike**".

The whole thing put into context the supposed difficulty of finding stories.

This was really hard.

I couldn't move for days!

Headline News

A golden rule of working in a freelance agency is never to answer the phone on a Friday evening.

Sadly, I broke this rule in 1987 when I was working at Cambrian News Agency on Charles Street in Cardiff. I was alone in the office, and the phone had been ringing for some time. I thought: 'Should I pick it up or shouldn't I?'.

Unfortunately, I did and on the other end it was the News Editor of a UK Sunday newspaper with a commission.

"I want you to do something for us", he drawled.

My heart sank. I should have known better than to answer that phone.

I could hear him puffing on his cigarette (everyone smoked in those days).

"A report has just come out naming the former Nazis who fled Germany, along with their addresses. Some of them came to Britain. One of them is near you – in Herefordshire (they had no idea of geography) I want you to get up there, find him and interview him."

That was it.

I had to think fast. Should I make up an excuse and say I was working on something else, or that there was no one available to go?

No – there was no alternative, I had to do it.

"Yes, of course", I said breezily. "We'd be happy to send someone (pretending we had a cast of thousands when there was only me in the office)".

So I drove to Herefordshire to find this man.

They were naturally all old people by then, and this person was living in an old people's home in the country. I found the home (by this time it was late at night) and I effectively broke into the building.

It wasn't illegal because it didn't involve damaging any windows or doors – it was all open and I just walked straight in. But it wouldn't have looked very good if the police had been called, and I said: "I am a reporter trying to find a man who worked for the Germans in the Second World War".

I quietly moved up the stairs to where I knew his room must be, and I knocked on the door. Incredibly he was still up.

"Hello," I said nervously. "My name is Phil Parry from xxxx newspaper, and I have a few questions to put to you".

I made the accusation – that he had been a prison guard for the Germans during World War II. What did he have to say for himself?

He accepted he was that person (he came from a Baltic state) but denied he had ever worked for the Germans.

"Er, thank you", I said haltingly with no idea what I should ask next.

I cleared my throat. "That will be all", I said, pretending I was from some official body because I knew I had to appear as though I knew what I was doing, even though I didn't have a clue.

I went back out as quietly as I came in, confident that my 'exclusive' would make a page lead in the Sunday newspaper: "Man denies he was a German prison guard in WWII" etc. My bosses would be extremely pleased, and the story would earn a lot of money.

I filed my copy and sat back and waited for the huge piece to appear, and the plaudits which would inevitably follow.

Unfortunately, it was the night of a terrible disaster and most of the planned stories were wiped out on the paper.

It made... a single paragraph!

Lies, Damned Lies etc.

Journalists never lie.

Or do they?

In 35 years in journalism I have only ever once made something up.

It is not something I am proud of – it was a complete and utter lie.

A complaint rightly, followed and I like to think I learned from that experience.

An old journalist friend of mine, who taught me a lot, once asked me many years ago what I thought was the single most important thing any journalist could have.

I came out with the usual stuff and said: "'integrity' or 'honesty', are the most important things".

"No," he answered, shaking his head.

"Those two things are important, but before them comes 'EXPERIENCE'".

He was quite right, and this experience taught me never again to make something up.

It happened when I was working for a freelance agency in Cardiff in the 1980s, called *Cambrian News Agency*.

We made money by finding stories and selling them to the UK papers in London.

On this occasion, I had heard that a famous astrologist was painting the rooms of his house according to the colours of the zodiac.

I didn't even know there were COLOURS of the zodiac, but there you go.

I knew the first thing the London papers would ask when they were confronted with my copy, would be: "Yes, but what colours ARE the rooms?".

So I made them up.

'Taurus, well, that's a bull, so that could be brown', I thought

'Leo, that's a lion, so that could be yellow and Scorpio, well, that could be any colour frankly, but some scorpions are gold' etc.

This was in the days before the internet, when you could find out anything with a few taps on your computer.

Of course, they were ALL wrong.

Justifiably, the astrologist rang up to complain, and after going first to the news desks of each paper, he eventually arrived at my news agency.

I waited nervously and could hear my boss (the same one who advised me about the importance of 'experience') trying to placate him.

"Yes, we're very sorry... it will never happen again... if you ever want a positive piece published about your charity work, then come to us", he said.

It must have worked because the complaint never went any further.

After putting the phone down, my boss advised me sternly: "That could have been very serious. It may sound funny but it is in fact libelous to suggest something like this. You made out this man does not know his astrology, because he was painting the rooms of his house in the wrong colours".

I was suitably chastened and swore it would never happen again.

To this day I have never made anything up.

I have been called "a lying bastard" by someone on his blog, and "biased" by somebody else on *Twitter*.

I may be a 'bastard', but I am certainly not a 'lying' or 'biased' one!

You must know your laws of libel.

It all comes down to the importance of 'experience'.

Names make News

For any journalist the first 'byline' in a newspaper is a major event.

To have 'by xxxx' under the headline, confers approval by the News Editor, a pat on the back for a job well done, and offers the prospect of being given good stories in future.

It is also something (most importantly) your mum can show to her neighbours!

The first byline in a 'national' (UK) newspaper is even more important.

These things were as rare as hen's teeth for reporters with a freelance agency (as I was, working for Cardiff's *Cambrian News Agency* in the mid 1980s,) where you picked up important stories and sold them to papers in London.

If your copy was used at all in the paper, then it was usually with the name of a staff person above it or with the addition of 'by a staff reporter'.

On this occasion, I had worked on a very sad story about a little girl who had died after being electrocuted when she touched the back of her father's fridge, which had been wrongly wired up.

I was 24 and, I am sorry to say, I could only see it as a good story.

The father and mother (who must have been grief stricken) would not speak, but I tracked down and interviewed shocked witnesses, and spoke to the police.

We pushed the story up to all the nationals, but one in particular, the *Daily Express*, came back wanting more details, which I duly found and provided.

The Express is a dreadful rag I now realise.

The other week, the first 10 stories on its website concerned the evils of Europe.

Then though it was a well-respected newspaper.

I worked on the story all day and I knew I was doing a good job.

"This will make a 'page lead'", I thought, "and we will get lots of money!".

In the late afternoon, news came back that the Editors on the Express were so pleased they were going to print it with a byline and asked for my name.

I was as pleased as punch.

I couldn't sleep that night, I was so excited!

The next day I rushed into the office early and waited for the plaudits to follow.

My two brothers were also journalists and they too would see my name, because the story would go out across the UK, not just in South Wales (I must confess there was an element of one-upmanship here).

My boss thundered up the stairs, as he did every morning, holding all the nationals in his arms, with me waiting at my desk like a cat on hot tin bricks.

"Have you seen it yet?" he said staring at me with a serious look.

"No, I haven't" I answered excitedly.

"Except in my dreams!"

He slapped the Express in front of me and I frantically flicked through the paper until I found the piece.

45

It was indeed a page lead.

"BY PHIL BARRY"...

Football Focus

During 10 years from 1989 as the presenter of the TV current affairs series *Week In, Week Out* on *BBC Wales,* I came across many intriguing sights.

This was after I was on *HTV Wales at Six.*

But perhaps no sight was as intriguing (indeed in my entire reporting career) as being close to a senior member of the Wales football management team during an international, and hearing what was said to players.

This was even more interesting than watching what happened to the former *Secretary of State for Wales,* Ron Davies or learning about the bizarre language of broadcasting!

None of my journalist exams in law and public administration had prepared me for this.

You have an idea the team talks are highly complex affairs, involving discussions about formation of the side, positional play and tactics.

This conversation, however, gave me an insight into something which was, well, anything but!

Week In, Week Out is sadly no more, but when I was lucky enough to be the face of the programme in the 1990s, we did many more episodes, and one was in North Wales, where we were filming.

After a heavy schedule, we managed to inveigle our way on to the touchline at *The Racecourse Ground* stadium in *Wrexham,* where *Wales* were playing *The Netherlands* – when international football games were played there – and I stood next to the *Wales* management team.

Instead of the complicated tactical instructions you imagine given to highly-paid footballers from their coaching staff, I heard something rather different.

"Go over to xxxx and tell him to start PLAYING!" was the direction.

I was then treated to the sight of a well-known, and highly-paid player going over to a team mate and passing the message on.

There were lots of raised arms and gesticulations, as this player pointed at the *Wales* management side and then pointed at his team mate.

After a few minutes of this, the player trotted back to the touchline to deliver the result to his bosses.

"He says he is FUCKING PLAYING!".

Broadcast News

A central part of when you go into broadcasting, is learning the language.

After a few months at the independent station, *HTV Wales,* I started on *BBC Wales Today* in 1987 and had to learn a completely new set of terms.

This was before I presented the now-axed *BBC Wales Current Affairs TV* programme '*Week In, Week Out*'.

A key word to learn was "pumping".

This had nothing to do with water, or anything more sniggery, but was in fact a crucial part of getting the pictures back to headquarters when you were out in the field.

It was easy enough to report a story if you were a reporter on a newspaper – you simply had to find a phone and 'file' the piece back to the newsroom.

In fact you would often look for the house with a telephone line (this was long before mobiles) and ask to use the owners' phone with a transfer-charge call.

But in broadcasting then it was completely different.

In television the pictures are, of course, a critical part of the report.

When I started in television you either had physically to drive the video tape (VT) to headquarters in Llandaff, Cardiff, or 'pump' the pictures back. This would often involve driving to a large mast in the middle of nowhere after you had covered the story, and transmitting the pictures back to headquarters, where they were then recorded by a friendly VT operator.

Now of course it is far easier to get the pictures on to TV screens, but then it wasn't.

The term I always remember was "Pumping from Blaenplwyf".

Blaenplwyf is a village in Ceredigion, near Aberystwyth, but crucially it also has a transmitting mast to send back your pictures.

"Pumping from Blaenplwyf" was one of the most unusual terms you had to know.

But there were plenty of others.

A friend of mine was completely stumped by the phrase "pumping from Norman Shaw".

These were in fact buildings in London which were used to send back the pictures of the *Political Correspondent* based there and record the 'links' to the radio recordings of the debate (television cameras were only allowed into the Commons in 1989). She thought, quite understandably, they were a person.

Apart from the almost impenetrable language, it was also crucial to learn HOW things were said.

Questions could be asked perfectly innocently, but to the hapless reporter or sub-editor, they would sound as if a terrible mistake had been made.

I remember coming back from the small studio in Llandaff after producing the *BBC Wales TV* lunchtime bulletin, and the News Transmission Assistant (NTA) would ask: "Phil, did YOU do lunchtime?"

At this my heart would always sink, thinking someone had already phoned in to complain, and I was in trouble.

But she would then go on to say: "Could you give me details of who we need to pay?" It was a perfectly reasonable request.

Language in journalism is everything.
But perhaps it means the most in broadcasting!

All in the Mind

This is a very difficult thing to write, but I feel it is important because mental illness should be spoken about as though it is any other condition.

When I left the *BBC* after 23 years, and when I was diagnosed with *Hereditary Spastic Paraplegia (HSP)*, I was told by a doctor I had severe depression.

A number of factors had combined to send me over the edge. For the first time in my career money wasn't squirted into my account every month, I was diagnosed with an incurable crippling disease and a friend of mine committed suicide.

As a result, I completely collapsed mentally.

I was on 'happy pills', had counselling, and I was treated by a specialist. I spent a year looking at old films on my computer, and I had no self-worth.

I became obsessed by the fact that I had no money coming in and I thought I had made a terrible mistake by going freelance.

Even small tasks were incredibly difficult, because I thought I would mess them up. I remember it took me all day to put up a basketball hoop for one of my kids.

Making tea for them should have been a simple job, but I found it incredibly hard. Any small criticism would be keenly felt, and ahead I could only see a future of blackness.

Ill-judged but well-meaning comments from friends or

family were no help either, such as: "I'm sure it is nothing", "You look fine". Or still worse: "What have you got to be depressed about?"

The point about mental illness is there is nothing to see. A broken arm or leg gets you sympathy, but a broken mind doesn't. It is, though, every bit as bad, if not worse.

The worst aspect was that I lost my sense of identity. I thought I was a *'BBC* journalist' rather than a journalist who worked at the *BBC*. Establishing *The Eye* was an important moment in helping to firm up that true identity.

I can tell you now that my HSP was as nothing compared with severe depression.

But the reason I am writing about this is not to elicit sympathy, but because I think it is not talked about enough. Depression needs to be in the open, and treated like any other serious illness, before it can be properly addressed.

I applaud the fact that the international rugby player Tom James could not be selected for a *Cardiff Blues* game against *Munster,* and that the reason was given as 'depression', alongside Alex Cuthbert who was recovering after knee surgery.

It is brilliant that mental illness is in the same category as any other debilitating condition.

But in many ways, it is still a 'taboo' subject, rather like cancer was 20 or 30 years ago.

For this reason, I feel strongly supportive of people who suffer a mental illness and I was shocked by the recent report which showed the poor level of care for children suffering with mental illness in Wales.

One girl told the authors of the report she had telephoned a mental help body, after finding her father dead on the kitchen floor, and that after almost a year she was still waiting for a call back.

A mental health unit in North Wales had to be closed down

after a camera smuggled on to the ward filmed patients crawling on the floor.

This was only exposed by a UK newspaper.

These things are appalling and should never be allowed to happen in the 21st century. Mental illness MUST be talked about and treated like any other serious illness.

I am sure it will be a great relief to all the crooks and corrupt politicians I have exposed over the years, that I am now fully back to fighting fitness.

Whenever people ask me what I do, I tell them I'm a 'professional troublemaker'!

Playing Politics

Covering politics has always been vital for the media.

The first election I covered was the 1987 General Election when I worked for *Cambrian News Agency* supplying stories for all the UK newspapers and broadcasters, as an extremely green 22 year old reporter.

I was stationed in the Caerphilly count and tasked with the responsibility of phoning the results back to my office, where they were then fed on to the wires.

This was the MP seat of the former *Secretary of State for Wales* Ron Davies, who was then a Labour opposition spokesman and a rising star, so that made it an important count.

Ron won his seat easily, which was always going to be the case, but I have several clear images of the night.

The key one concerns the Liberal Party (as they were then called) candidate Michael Butlin.

I always remember he very ostentatiously opened what looked like a bottle of bubbly during the count.

This was highly ironic in the circumstances as he came in a distant third!

Mr Butlin slipped into relative obscurity, but Ron's political career soared from then on, yet crashed spectacularly.

He spearheaded the Welsh pro-devolution campaign in 1997 (a vote which I also covered in a draughty leisure centre), and the referendum was won with the narrowest of margins –

50.3 per cent to 49.7 per cent.

As a journalist I watched what happened next avidly, and our paths crossed many times in the years that followed, including being rung at home by Ron.

One of our meetings included being briefed by him in his London office when he was Welsh Secretary, after I had interviewed him on another matter, during my years presenting the now-defunct *BBC Wales TV* current affairs programme, *Week In, Week Out*.

On other occasions he was a regular panelist on a weekly debate programme I hosted on *BBC Radio Wales* called *The People's Assembly*.

He was a fine contributor and always answered the questions well.

First Ron was the 'architect of devolution' in Wales, but then in the media, he was the 'architect of his own destruction'.

In October 1998 journalists were summoned to Downing Street and told that Ron had resigned as Welsh Secretary after admitting to the Prime Minister "a serious lapse of judgment" on *Clapham Common* the previous evening but denied any sexual element.

He was the first of Tony Blair's ministers to resign.

Ron claimed he had been robbed by a Rastafarian man, whom he had just met but was about to dine with, in the presence of others.

His car, telephone, wallet and *House of Commons* pass were stolen, and six people were arrested.

Ron went on television to apologise for his "moment of madness", while on his hand was scrawled the word "sorry".

But it continued, and for a young journalist from South Wales it was extraordinary to see – like watching a car crash in slow motion.

The Sun reported that Ron had engaged in a sex act in

daylight with a stranger at Tog Hill in 2003.

This was a picnic area eight miles North of Bath in Somerset, and it was only 17 days after his third wife had given birth to their first child.

The newspaper had received a tip-off and sent a photographer.

The published pictures showed Ron leaving the bushes, but they claimed unpublished pictures captured the act.

He told the Sun: "These allegations are completely false and without substance."

Ron said to other journalists: "I have actually been there when I have been watching badgers".

But he told the House of Commons, cryptically: "We are what we are.

"We are all different, the product of both our genes and our experiences."

In June 1999, Ron had disclosed he was bisexual and said he was having psychiatric treatment to curb a "compulsive" quest for risk.

In the 2008 local elections he was elected to Caerphilly council, as an independent councillor.

In fact, he has never been far from the news.

In September 2016, footage emerged apparently showing him placing (or as he said, clearing) rocks and logs on Caerphilly Mountain, after a row over how mountain bikers were using the area.

So that was it.

One of the most talented Welsh politicians of his generation was brought down by scandal and hubris.

I was reminded of that quote from Hamlet: "The lady doth protest too much, methinks".

As for Mr Butlin – I don't know what became of him. As a journalist I suppose I should know these things!

Court in the Act

Sometimes crime stories culminate in a court case which you must also report.

Phil as a judge in cartoon by Wyn on The Eye

In fact, *Magistrates Court* and *Crown Court* are a regular haunt of the reporter, where they appear every day on the 'diary' of events which should be covered.

They are up there along with politics as sources of news for all journalists.

In my early years in the 1980s as a cub reporter on *The South Wales Echo*, there were dedicated reporters for the 'mags court' in Cardiff, as well as for the *Crown Court*, although they aren't there now.

But we were also sent along to help them out on big cases.

This was long before I presented the now-axed *BBC Wales* TV current affairs series *Week In, Week Out*, although knowledge of the law and the court system came in extremely handy then, too.

I often thought the 'mags court' would be a great place to stage a drama or even a sit-com because all human life is there.

You had to know what you could and couldn't say – but it was different to the libel laws we were taught.

In courts the (usually young and male) individual would be surrounded by the family and solicitor.

He would be up for nicking cars, or on an 'affray' charge after a fight in the street when the pubs closed.

Usually he would be in his best suit, so you could always spot the accused a mile off.

After an initial hearing the more serious crimes were kicked upstairs where they would be heard in *Crown Court* (they are on different sites now), although the bog-standard cases were dealt with in 'mags'.

But I came to question the value of throwing the book at some of these people.

A serious case which went to the *Crown Court* and I remember well, was of a father who was on child neglect charges.

He had left his children alone in the bath while he went to his usual club and had a drink

The children had managed to pull a hairdryer into the water and, appallingly, electrocuted themselves.

The man had done a terrible thing by leaving them in the

bath to go for a pint and I would never have done it.

Yet he cut a terribly forlorn figure in the dock.

He had lost his two children through his own awful mistake, and here he was on charges in court.

There is an argument, which I respect, that he needed to be punished by the state and held up as an example of something which should never be done.

But there is also an argument that justice is not served by punishing someone who has done a devastating thing, and is grieving for his two dead children after it.

Yet of course, I dutifully wrote the copy that he was a 'monster' who had killed his children and was in court.

Even as I filed my report to the 'copy taker' I wondered.

I was 22 at the time, and you come across a lot of awful things like this.

I remember covering a succession of child abuse cases, and all of these had the 'monster' treatment too – rightly.

Even I was starting to feel a little sick by the end of the third one.

But you had to toughen up quickly, as a young reporter, and "get your knees brown" as my old News Editor used to say!

Fate Twisted

In 1987 I worked as a reporter on *HTV Wales at Six* in the Pontcanna newsroom in Cardiff.

It was a very happy place to start your career in broadcasting.

In fact, I liked it so much that when I secured a better job at *BBC Wales* I approached the management at HTV to offer my services.

There was a 'community' atmosphere in the newsroom and I developed many friends there, who are still with me today.

The small 'club' in the grounds of HTV was known as 'Grumpy's grotto' and could always be relied on for a drink – even if the beer wasn't very good there.

You could get a better pint across the road at *'The Halfway'*.

This was in the days when the pub was divided into three bars, and we usually colonised the small corner one after work.

There was also a cat which lived in the newsroom, but we left the window open so that it could go outside.

On one occasion the cat upset his saucer of milk all over the presenter's suit before he went on air.

He had to clean up before he presented the news!

For our reports the pictures were cut first, then the commentary was 'dubbed' on to the piece in a special studio.

This process was slightly longer, but the finished product always looked better, so we thought ourselves rather superior.

Broadcasting in those days progressed in jumps rather than gradually and in a linear process.

When I joined, we were on tape (which was thought to be cutting edge then), but only a few years before we were way behind and the reports had been on film, which of course needed to be developed before they went on air.

There was still talk of one heroic individual who drove down from North Wales every day, with the film to be developed in his car, of the story for that evening's news.

No story could be covered after lunch time because that would not be enough time to film it, drive down from North Wales to Cardiff, develop the film and get it on air!

When I was offered the job at *BBC Wales Today,* I went in to see the then Editor of *Wales at Six.*

"I've been offered a job at the BBC", I said.

"But I'd much rather stay here, do you have anything coming up, even on less money?".

"I'm afraid not", he answered.

"It's a very difficult time – you had better take the job at the BBC"

So I left for *BBC Wales* in Llandaff, where I stayed for 23 years.

I was promoted several times, broke a number of stories and was lucky enough to win numerous awards.

I presented the BBC Wales TV Current Affairs programme Week In, Week Out for 10 years until 1999.

It has now been axed after 53 years and been replaced by the strap 'BBC Wales Investigates' on 'big' stories.

On BBC 1, I was the reporter on several Panorama programmes, while on BBC 2, I presented Public Eye and Newsnight films.

I hosted numerous live radio shows.

But it could all have been so different if that Editor at HTV had said 'yes'!

Another Letter of the Law

Every journalist worth his or her salt must know the laws of libel.

Broadly speaking, being obnoxious does not defame someone, but undermining the reputation of that person, or the ability to earn a living, may do.

This is the bedrock of journalism, and luckily knowing this has earned me many awards.

You can say the First Minister of Wales is a bastard (although he is not) because that could be defended as *Fair Comment* (or *Honest Comment* as it is now known), but you cannot say he is a cheating bastard unless you have very strong evidence (but there is none, because he is NOT a cheat – let me make that perfectly clear!).

Over the years I have been involved in countless legal cases – covering them, defending them and prosecuting them.

The regular Tuesday evening *BBC Wales Television* current affairs series I presented for 10 years from 1989, *Week In, Week Out,* has been axed after 53 years, and replaced by the strap 'BBC Wales Investigates' on 'big' stories, but on Mondays we would invariably be joined by a corporation lawyer to check every word of the programme script, as well as every frame of the film.

People who had no idea of the law would complain about

things that were NEVER in the programme!

After libel cases I have won large amounts of money and lost large amounts of money for my then-employer when the court has not accepted my lawyer's defence.

The media landscape, and indeed the law itself, changes all the time; but the fundamentals do not.

Newspaper circulations may be plunging but legal basics are unchanged.

A piece on *Facebook* or *Twitter* is governed by the same laws of libel as if it were an item on *BBC Wales Today* or a page-lead in the *Western Mail*.

People do not seem to be aware of this though, and say the most appalling things on social media, and some of it is libelous.

A widespread dissemination comes into it too.

I have been called wrongly a "lying bastard" and "biased" as well as "misogynistic" on the internet.

The full text of the 'biased' tweet came after a story about a woman Welsh Assembly Member (AM) and was: "Severed links with @WalesEye (our *Twitter* name) years ago. Unfunny, biased, personal, superficial, mysoginistic (sic), out of touch &bitter. That's WalesEye, not me".

Now, you can probably get away with most of this stuff although it is obnoxious ('unfunny' for example can be defended as *Honest Comment*) but 'biased' and 'misogynistic' (even if misspelt) are quite different.

Possessing the knowledge of what separates these things is crucial.

To call a journalist 'biased' (let alone a 'misogynist') is probably the worst thing you can say, because it undermines that person's ability to earn a living.

66

If you are seen as not being neutral, then people will refuse to come to you with the other side of the story.

Also, this was by someone who has a fairly large following on *Twitter*.

As to the first 'bastard' comment – that is probably acceptable (I hold my hands up to being a bastard on the doorstep sometimes!) but a 'liar' is something you should never say about a journalist unless, again, you have very strong evidence.

On the other hand, this blog was seen by virtually no one, and the dissemination would not have been widespread – so I did nothing about it.

The second insult on *Twitter* was another matter entirely.

I went straight to my libel lawyer who consulted a specialist barrister.

We threatened to sue and a full apology as well as retraction were duly published.

But knowing about these rules seems to be a scarce commodity, and over the years we have endured numerous threats of legal action from people who do not understand what they are saying.

None of these threats have come to anything.

Real journalism is much harder than just writing about '19 mouth-watering street food dishes' as the Editor of one news website advised a reader.

In pursuing it you also need to be aware that other issues are key in libel law past and present.

In 1921 an interesting court case took place after a strange incident in Littlehampton.

A woman called Edith Swan had been sending poison pen letters to neighbours she hated.

Here is an extract of one of them: "You bloody fucking piss country whores go and fuck your cunt. It's your drain that stinks not your fish box. Yo fucking dirty sods. You are as bad as your whore neybor."

But the jury in the libel trial of Swan refused to convict her because she had an education (unbelievably) after a judge's direction, and another jury later wrongly convicted an ill-educated woman called Rose Gooding, who was sentenced to 12 months in prison with hard labour.

She was fully exonerated afterwards.

My point is that the legal aspect may change (and sometimes the law is an ass!) but the fundamentals do not.

You cannot go around saying anything, and publishing anything about people – if only social media users knew that!

Broadcasting your Fears...

Here are some tips for you.

If you are ever in the unfortunate position of facing aggressive questions during a television or radio interview – disarm the interviewer.

Come over as friendly and reasonable.

It works every time.

Also – if the audience believes the allegedly guilty party is reasonable and has a fair point, the interviewer will be put on the back foot.

After being a journalist in the BBC for 23 years, I feel now is the time to divulge some of the secrets!

Never, EVER, storm out of an interview, because you immediately look guilty.

The former Defence Secretary John (now Sir John) Nott notoriously did it in a fit of pique when he took exception to the apparently innocuous phrase "here today and gone tomorrow politician".

His career never fully recovered.

Storming out like this is extremely rare, but it has happened to me a few times during my interviews.

You always know you are on to a winner when you sense this is about to happen.

'Just one more question will push him (and it usually is a him) *over the edge and he will be gone'* you think!

All the reporter has to do then is shout questions at the disappearing back, like "why won't you answer the question Mr xxxx ?".

Two of the 'walk-outs' were during filming for the now-defunct *BBC Wales* Current Affairs series *Week In Week Out (WIWO).*

One was in an interview with a dodgy Government minister, and another was when I confronted a fraudster with the truth about her claims.

I think it is a vital role for journalists to hold to account those with influence over people's lives.

It is why I am deeply upset that WIWO has now been axed after 53 years.

I could earn a fortune offering this sort of advice to corporations or Governments, yet here I am giving it away for free!

Whatever the rights or wrongs of the case you are investigating, remember that the sympathies of the audience can all-too easily be transferred from the interviewer to the person on the other end of the microphone.

If the reporter is on location it does not help that he or she is often out of shot or just represented by a voice.

That too makes the whole thing appear unfair in the minds of people watching or listening.

But techniques which unsettle the interviewer are the best ones.

Long before I started *The Eye,* a senior Welsh politician was before me and the TV camera on *BBC Wales Today,* after slogans had been daubed on a Government building.

He hadn't done it, but he was defending those who had, and I was preparing to give him a hard time.

Before the interview started, he leant over and touched me.
"That's a nice tie," he whispered.
"Where did you get it?"

I was of course, completely floored and stuttered out my 'aggressive' questions.

On another occasion I filmed a report for *BBC 2 Newsnight* about the noises coming from a home for disabled people.

The manager of the home was in front of me, but before the camera was rolling he said: "You look rather tired, are you all right?".

Again, I was completely flummoxed, and my questions missed their target.

Another tactic is to keep your answers very short.

A curt "yes" or "no" is a nightmare for interviewers because it throws the ball back into his or her court.

There is no onus on you to fill space, but the thought of 'dead air' is an awful one for any professional in TV or radio.

Learning these techniques is almost as important as our journalism on *The Eye* where we have, for example, uncovered a crooked South Wales property 'expert' now selling luxury villas in Spain, and a criminal who was employed at one Welsh Management School, despite being jailed in America for more than four years after a huge fraud.

It is certainly more important than the recommendation by one litigious Welsh website Editor who advised that the way to break into journalism was by writing lists about the best street food, although not as vital as knowing about the law.

So my advice is simple:
KEEP IT SHORT AND BE NICE!

Notes for Life

It seems old fashioned reporting skills may be staging a comeback.

Taking down notes of an interview in a notebook is less easy to hack into than using new technology, and the system is more reliable.

More and more people see shorthand as essential to progressing in journalism, possibly ensuring the quotes taken down are accurate.

When I started in journalism 35 years ago it was an essential part of a reporter's tool kit.

Piers Morgan may be an acquired taste but his views are certainly important to all journalists.

He was a former Editor of the *Daily Mirror* who is now a TV presenter and was named the most influential journalist on social media by the *UK Press Gazette*.

He has championed the use of shorthand.

He said: "Having an ability to take fast contemporaneous handwritten notes as a back-up to technology is invaluable."

"I still use Teeline (a shorthand system) on *Good Morning Britain* during a big breaking news story live on air when I want to make a note of a powerful quote and repeat it very soon afterwards".

Mr Morgan also offered a cautionary tale about relying on technology: "Tape recorders are great until they don't work, as I once discovered when I interviewed Rod Stewart for an hour and later could only hear my voice..."

Teeline, as opposed to the more challenging *Pitman* variation, celebrated its 50th anniversary recently.

It was developed by the Bradford schoolteacher James Hill, who wanted to come up with a quicker and more straightforward method of note-taking, and he began experimenting as early as 1939.

Decades later he saw some promising results when he taught experimental classes to journalism trainees.

In 1968 the system was recommended to the *National Council for the Training of Journalists* (NCTJ), and in November that year its shorthand consultant Harry Butler wrote: "We have on our hands a shorthand breakthrough which should solve longstanding shorthand problems."

"I have never known a shorthand system that can produce such good results in so short a time."

Since then, learning to do shorthand has become something of a rite of passage for every would-be journalist as he or she struggles to reach 100 words per minute – the industry standard.

The star footballer Cristiano Ronaldo won damages from the *Daily Telegraph*, after quotes published about him were deemed to be inaccurate.

The shorthand of the journalist in question was regarded as so sloppy that his reporting could not be accurate.

Hacking into new technology on social media is very much in the news now, and it has provided another spur to the reporter conducting a notebook interview using a pen and paper.

It has emerged that personal details of about 150 million users of the *MyFitnessPal* app were compromised in one of the biggest hacks in history, according to its parent company.

The US sportswear brand *Under Armour* said user names,

email addresses and scrambled passwords were among the stolen data, and it urged customers to change their passwords immediately.

The social media giant *Facebook* is at the centre of a scandal about the use of data by the political consultancy *Cambridge Analytica*.

Facebook believes information on up to 87 million people was improperly shared with *Cambridge Analytica* – many more than previously disclosed – and about 1.1 million of them are UK-based.

British and US lawyers have launched a joint class action against them, along with two other companies, for allegedly misusing personal data.

Facebook chief Mark Zuckerberg said: "clearly we should have done more, and we will going forward".

Perhaps journalists should go forward too – with a notebook and pen!

Secrets of the Trade

Unfortunately, as an investigative reporter I have had to use subterfuge many times to get at the truth.

Over the years I have worn hidden cameras, posed as a long-lost relative, secretly recorded people, and kept a whirring tape recorder in my bag.

I have even presented myself on the doorstep of an interviewee knowing she thought I was a policeman, in order to get the information needed – although I stress I have never impersonated a police officer as this is against the law.

Bizarrely when I was working for *BBC* Panorama long before my HSP set in, I rang up a leading Cardiff barrister for a quote and NOT recording the conversation, he said: "This is being recorded".

So I replied: "No don't worry – I am not recording".

"No", he said. "I AM recording it"!

This remarkable interchange stresses that the line between comedy and drama is very finely drawn, and on the same Panorama programme I was treated to more classic examples of this.

To record one particular interview (with a serving and potentially murderous police officer) I wore a hidden camera in my tie which became very hot.

I kept having to move my tie otherwise the heat would have become unbearable on my chest!

The interview was being conducted at a safe location in

Neath where I knew the windows were on one side.

I hared up the stairs with my producer in order to sit with my back to the window, so the police officer would have to take the seat with his back to the wall and the light on him.

I knew that if he had taken the seat next to the window, the light behind him would have rendered the shot useless.

I remember thinking to myself this is so ridiculous it would make a brilliant sit-com!

In order to do any secret filming at *The BBC* you had to surmount all sorts of bureaucratic hurdles and get the agreement of your Editor.

You also became aware of how useless technology can be in these circumstances.

On that *BBC Panorama* programme, both my producer and I were wearing hidden tie cameras, but his broke down so we were reliant on mine which thankfully kept working despite my repeated moving of the tie!

My producer wore glasses and he told me once that interviewees often thought a recording device was fitted into his spectacles case!

It never was.

You will be glad to know we secured the interview with the police officer and he effectively confessed to murder.

Knowledge of how to do these sorts of things legally is almost as important for journalists as knowing the libel laws.

Sadly, it seems some others in journalism do not know those laws.

Luckily using these kinds of techniques, though, has brought me many awards and the risks were worthwhile.

I was always oblivious to any danger but looking back I suppose it was ever-present.

I recall on one occasion *The BBC* paid to have my home wired for intruders and panic buttons installed at my bedside and on the landing. In fairness to the organisation, officials even paid for a security expert to come from London to talk to me.

I remember he was most concerned to know whether I had a regular pattern of movements, and who and from where the children were picked up after school.

I had to go X-directory (I still am) and have my car number plate blurred out on programmes, because it was in a couple of shots.

My family are only hearing about these things now!

Long before I started *The Eye,* the Editor of another TV programme I worked on, said I was the bravest journalist he had ever known, but I can honestly say these risks never entered my mind.

You just did your job.

Pay Down

Most journalism is extremely badly-paid.

When I started more than 35 years ago I was on a salary of less than £5,000 a year.

This was when I was training as a cub reporter on *The South Wales Echo.*

We knew that economising was the order of the day, and every trip in the beat up 'office car', which we shared with reporters on *The Western Mail,* had to be accounted for.

Our low pay was nominally 'topped up' by expenses (or 'exes').

This practice of 'using' expenses to subsidise the low salary, was completely illegal of course because it gave us untaxed money.

It was unsaid, but we all knew, that everyone had a certain level and, as the most junior member of the newsroom, mine was about £12 a week.

I remember one week I had the audacity to bump up my 'claim' to £14 but the News Editor, Stuart 'Minto' Minton took it down again, saying: "Oh, no, no. We can't have this".

When I moved to a Cardiff freelance agency on Charles Street called *Cambrian News Agency* in 1986 the situation was little better.

I had a slight pay rise, but my starting salary was still only £6,000 a year.

When I moved into broadcasting a year later, however, the picture was very different.

On *BBC Wales Today,* my salary immediately soared to an unheard-of £12,500 a year with generous expenses.

When I transferred to the now-defunct TV Current Affairs series *Week In, Week Out* my pay went up again.

The expenses system at the *BBC* (now thankfully altered) was ripe for exploitation.

You could claim a standard amount for lunch or evening meal (about £6 and £9) even if you had only eaten a sandwich, and no receipts were required.

So you could pay for a cheapo egg and cress sandwich with a cup of coffee standing up in a greasy-spoon cafe to keep going while you were out filming, yet claim huge amounts of money for it.

For overnight stays it was the same system.

You would charge a standard amount if you had stayed in a flea-pit B and B, or even if you headed home and had a free night in your own bed.

This was known as 'doing a flyer'.

You could also claim for 'wet-weather' gear.

I remember doing this in the middle of summer and I got a call from an official in the Personnel Department (as it then was) who had picked up on the claim, saying that no one had ever done this before!

Network television was even worse (or better depending on your perspective!).

I remember when I was filming for *BBC Panorama* in Italy, I was picked up from the airport in a chauffeur-driven *Mercedes-Benz* and I was then whisked to the Rome office!

Back in London, we used to have '*BBC* cars' waiting outside our offices to take us to interviews.

On *BBC Public Eye* I had to film in America, and I was

booked into a hotel room in Little Rock, Arkansas, which had a sitting-room AND a bedroom.

This has all now again thankfully changed; receipts must be provided and everything justified.

Quite right too.

Meanwhile on *The Eye* I still do the same journalism of challenging those in authority but make virtually no money whatsoever.

I feel like I am back at square one!

Prize Decision

Congratulations must be paid to the team from the *BBC Wales TV* current affairs series *'Week In, Week Out' (WIWO)* for winning a top award in the *BAFTA Cymru* ceremony.

This is hugely ironic as the programme has been scrapped.

A new strand *'BBC Wales Investigates' (BWI)* for occasional 'major' stories was formally announced with huge fanfare to replace it with the same journalists.

The irony has not been lost on critics, including me after presenting WIWO for 10 years from 1989. This is quite incredible and only serves to underline what a crass mistake it was to get rid of WIWO – a regular weekly TV current affairs series is important.

BBC Wales Director, Rhodri Talfan Davies said at the time of the announcement it came as part of "the biggest single investment in Welsh services for over 20 years".

But investment in Current Affairs television in recent years has apparently been a scarce commodity. On network *BBC TV, Panorama* is now a shadow of its former self, and *Rough Justice* as well as *Public Eye* have gone altogether. On *ITV, World in Action, This Week* and *First Tuesday* have all disappeared.

In the last run of WIWO only five programmes were produced as the series became less important.

A UK 'brand' and marketing expert told us: "It is extremely

dangerous to get rid of an established brand. Many of our customers are idiots and tell us they want to dump a long-established brand to set up a new one. We have to tell them it is complete madness".

Winning awards, such as the one at the *BAFTA Cymru* ceremony, was a regular feat for WIWO.

In the programme's hey day in the 1980s and 1990s, a skeleton staff provided 30 regular programmes a year on Tuesday nights plus 'specials'. Vital evidence was uncovered, such as in one programme called *A Night To Remember* on the Cardiff Newsagent Three, which led to the release from prison of three men who had been wrongly convicted of murder, and many of these programmes went on to win awards such as at the *Royal Television Society* as well as with *BAFTA Cymru*.

One WIWO still features near the top of internal documents for all-time best viewing figures, and the programme successfully withstood numerous legal threats.

Despite this, WIWO was axed after 53 years before BWI was launched.

The last regular presenter of WIWO, Tim Rogers, spoke of how central the programme was, and in a magazine article on the programme's 50th birthday said: "WIWO as we affectionately call it, is a broadcasting institution. Fifty years old this week it is one of the longest running current affairs programmes on British TV. It is certainly the oldest and one of the most respected in Wales."

But great respect in Wales did not save WIWO from the axe, and I was outraged.

I told the *Western Mail* when the closure of WIWO hit the headlines: "It is absurd to suggest that putting a label on a story like '*BBC Wales Investigates*' in any way compensates for getting rid of a regular weekly current affairs strand which had been going for many years, like *Week In Week Out*. It never works – they tried to say the same when they got rid of

Public Eye on BBC 2. *Public Eye Investigations* was never heard of again".

But the BBC remained defiant. A spokesperson told us: "*BBC Wales Investigates* is a hard-hitting current affairs strand, which produces investigative pieces for all platforms – TV, radio and online. As it stands, it (*the first and at that point only programme*) has set a new record for any story published by the global BBC News website for the time spent reading an article".

Yet the contrast with *ITV Wales* is marked.

A spokesperson at the broadcaster said their Current Affairs series *Wales This Week* was given a lengthy run and programmes were broadcast in peak times.

"We provide 24 episodes a year at 8 pm", he said. "*Wales This Week* is a key brand for us."

But it seems WIWO was not a key brand for *BBC Wales*.

A debate series examining the issues of the day was axed after just one year and at a cost of around £1 million. Tenders have been published for a production company to deliver a new debate programme to take over from *The Hour*. Yet viewers had described it as "necessary" and even *BBC Wales* have admitted to *The Eye* it "capture(d) the mood of the nation".

The Hour was a monthly debate show which toured Wales. On the programme's *Facebook* page viewers were very complimentary about a transmission called 'Debating the future of the NHS'. One said it was an "excellent discussion" another that it provided "great insight" and that it was "enlightening" while a further viewer said it was "a necessary entity to air the views of the public in Wales". The BBC had seemed equally enthusiastic, stressing that "In 60 minutes, 60 people get the chance to explore a topic in depth and hold politicians to account".

83

Yet the *TaxPayers' Alliance* told *The Eye* after its closure was revealed: "The BBC cannot be this profligate and not expect to face serious and legitimate criticism from licence fee payers".

No Smoke without Fire

Major cultural changes are extremely rare, but they do happen.

The *First World War* is the root cause of one of them – and its ending over 100 years ago, had unforeseen ramifications.

When I started in journalism 35 years ago almost everyone in my newsroom smoked and you could cut the air with a knife.

The reporter opposite me on the paper smoked small cigars, and another always had extremely long cigarettes so he could linger on doorsteps while he smoked them!

But now smoking is frowned upon.

It is no longer allowed in pubs or cafes, and you regularly see a gaggle of hardened nicotine addicts outside buildings.

The first question you were asked on my *Thomson Regional Newspapers (TRN)* training course in *Newcastle* where I was sent as a cub reporter, was "who here smokes?" and an ash tray was placed with great gravitas on his or her desk.

When I was lucky enough to be appointed the presenter of the *BBC Wales Television* Current Affairs programme, *Week In, Week Out (WIWO)* I was privileged to interview Sir Richard Doll.

Unfortunately, WIWO has now been ditched in favour of '*BBC Wales Investigates*'.

But the programme exposed me to the knowledge that if anyone deserves a statue in towns and cities around the UK it is Sir Richard, because his work saved millions of lives.

HE should be immortalised in stone, rather than erecting statues of men on horses!

Sir Richard was an epidemiologist and the team he led discovered the link between smoking and lung cancer.

He explained to me how they could not work out why there was a sudden spike in lung cancer deaths in the 1920s, and they pursued a number of different avenues, before all of them proved dead ends.

Among the possible causes, as they thought, was that the growth in lung cancer was because it was linked to the process of putting down new road surfaces – which was happening a lot in the 1920s.

But eventually they worked out it was not this.

In the end they established that the cause of the growth in lung cancer was because of the *First World War*.

At the beginning, in 1914, ordinary soldiers were recruited who smoked clay pipes.

These, though, were far more susceptible to being seen by eagle-eyed enemy snipers when they were in the trenches, so the soldiers quickly switched to cigarettes which were easier to hide and extinguish.

When the war finally finished in 1918 the demobbed soldiers brought their cigarette habit home and it quickly became de rigueur to smoke cigarettes, which are, of course, far more effective in delivering carcinogenic smoke into the lungs than clay pipes.

So that, Sir Richard explained, was behind the sudden upsurge in lung cancer cases in the 1920s and he went on to write several books trying to publicise his work.

But even though the link between cigarettes and lung cancer was known about early in the 20th century, it would be decades before action was taken.

A smoking ban in England, making it illegal to smoke in all

enclosed work places, only came into force on July 1, 2007 as a consequence of the Health Act of 2006.

Similar bans had already been introduced by politicians in the rest of the United Kingdom – in Scotland on March 26, 2006, Wales on April 2, 2007 and Northern Ireland on April 30, 2007.

Smoking is by far the biggest preventable cause of cancer.

It accounts for more than 1 in 4 UK cancer deaths, and 3 in 20 cancer cases.

It has been reported that major US tobacco companies were to publish and broadcast messages that clearly stated they designed their products to be more addictive, even while knowing their health effects were deadly.

So, Sir Richard has been responsible for saving more lives than anyone else.

His name should be known more widely and his work should be celebrated everywhere.

If nothing else, he is the reason why you can see properly now in newsrooms.

And the *First World War* of course!

Caning Canned

My interest in journalism can be traced back to my education because this is when it began. But I pay only a muted tribute to one of my old science teachers in the boys' school I attended who has just died, because his death has thrown into stark relief the physical abuse suffered by children.

AW 'Bill' Griffiths was in charge of *Chemistry* at *Monmouth School* from 1962 to 1993 and has died of old age.

The funeral notice from the *Old Monmothian Club* says he: "passed away peacefully in his sleep on Sunday 4th November 2018".

But 'peace' was never a word we associated with 'Bill Griff'.

He was a teacher who physically assaulted children. I clearly remember being hit in the head by him because, along with the rest of the class, I was 'marching' into the *Chemistry* lesson and making a noise on the wooden floor.

'Bill Griff's' attack sent me spinning into the hallway where I had to spend the rest of the lesson. I saw stars.

He was also housemaster of the small boys boarding house called *St James'*, where the children went before, they were assigned to their allotted senior houses. He hit boys there too.

I remember a young friend of mine confided in me that 'Bill Griff' had told him that although he caned other boys, he would not touch him because he liked him. These were children of eleven or twelve years old.

Another master used to keep an old 'dap' or plimsole in his

bag to hit the boys if they misbehaved. Before the beating took place, he would often ask the class to vote on whether the dap should be used and, of course, boys being boys, they invariably voted for the assault to take place. This teacher was a genuine fascist and wore a black arm band to school the day that Franco died.

A class vote before the beating happened to me once (I was always getting beaten for day dreaming or talking in class) and everyone voted for me to be dapped except, to his eternal credit, my best friend at the time.

A biology teacher used to beat boys on their behinds using a large pair of wooden protractors with the word 'IDIOT' scrawled on the instrument backwards in chalk. After the beating took place the victim would have 'IDIOT' in chalk the right way round on his backside.

On another occasion when I was misbehaving in the dinner queue, a master came up behind me, hurled me down a flight of stone stairs and held me up against a wall. I was only twelve.

But these assaults had a terrible effect on us as children, which lasted until we were adults.

My best mate in school (the one who voted for me not to be beaten, and who is still a friend of mine today) only told me earlier this year of how he was caned by the Headmaster for riding his bike in the wrong part of school. He is in his 50s.

He found the experience painful, and so deeply humiliating he did not tell me at the time. Only now has he told me, even though I have seen him countless times since we both left Monmouth.

Before I arrived at the school even superior *Prefects* (called *'Monitors'*) were allowed to beat younger children. The satirical film *'If'* was actually spot on. That appalling phrase "it never did me any harm" could not be further from the truth.

Monmouth School is a second division independent or 'public' school and certainly not in the same league as Eton or

Westminster. Their motto is "Serve And Obey".

As pupils we came to know that motto well, because if we stepped out of line we were regularly beaten.

Apart from the abuse, it was a very traditional school with an ever-present air of menace.

Prefects were allowed to dispense summary justice in the form of *'drills'* which were basically orders to do lines after school, and if your work was not up to scratch you were given a *'detention'* to write a short essay on Saturdays before watching the first 15 play rugby, which was obligatory.

As a special privilege, *prefects* (which I was never appointed as I was a bit of a rebel) were allowed to push in the dinner queue and walk on a central bit of grass.

I breathed a huge sigh of relief when I left after seven years to go to university.

Thankfully, now, the boys are extremely well-taught at *Monmouth School* and physical punishment is not allowed. But when I went there it was effectively a *Grammar School* with pretensions, and I was admitted on a *'Direct Grant'*.

I always remember we were not allowed to call it a *'Grammar School'* because that was rather looked down on (although it never did *Manchester Grammar School* any harm!) but everything has changed today.

In state-run schools, and in independent schools where some of the funding came from state coffers, beatings were outlawed in 1986, following a 1982 ruling by the *European Court of Human Rights* that such punishment could not be administered without parental consent, and that a child's "right to education" could not be infringed. In other independent schools, it was banned in 1998 (in England and Wales), 2000 (in Scotland) and 2003 (in Northern Ireland).

At the time a total ban was being prepared to come into force in Wales the NSPCC Cymru/Wales said: "We welcome the steps being taken by the *Welsh Government* towards removing the defence of 'reasonable punishment'. Every child deserves equal protection under the law and should be protected from such draconian forms of discipline. It is wrong that a defense which does not exist in a case of common assault against an adult can be used to justify striking a child."

Most countries around the world have made it unlawful to assault children.

In Argentina, for example, it was banned in 1813, but was re-legalised in 1817 and punishments by caning lasted for decades. Yet all corporal punishment finally became prohibited through a law in 2014 which came into force in January 2016.

A friend of mine who lives opposite, attended *Monmouth School* in the 1960s when the physical abuse by teachers on children was even worse.

He hates the school even more than I do, and we meet up regularly to talk about the beatings, which we call our 'therapy sessions'.

At one of them he told me: "We can't tell our wives because they simply wouldn't understand. I can only talk to you about this".

These 'therapy sessions' are likely to continue for many years to come...

Publishing on *The Eye* these memories of my school days prompted a huge response from readers.

One reader told us: "It was legalised assaults. My school – a comp – was the same. One teacher hit us with a wooden T-square – that thing you used to draw lines in technical drawing – with another square taped to it. It would hit you and then the other one would swing round and hit you a second time a fraction of a second later. What ingenuity!".

Another said: "The teacher used a slipper on us he kept in his desk". A different reader told us: "Our teacher was a real sadist who rubbed our knuckles on the radiator if we did something wrong in class, which was extremely painful".

A further reader of *The Eye* said: "I had a headmaster who never came out of his office. People went to see him for two reasons – a) to deliver his newspaper *(The Times)*, b) to receive the cane/slipper. Before he hit you, he'd ask if you deserved it. If you said no, you had to remain in his office until such time as you made your confession. I think Stalin's NKVD used similar tactics in the 1930s".

A Good Story

It all came down to a book.

I was being interviewed by a panel of senior managers for my first job as a temporary 'Sub-Editor' on *Wales Today* at *The BBC* in 1987 and it was going really badly.

They called these interviews 'boards' then, as they tried to emulate the Civil Service system, before things really began to change.

I answered all the questions wrongly and I could sense that those on the board had taken against me.

In those days they asked you what book you were reading.

I answered, quite truthfully, it was *The Ragged Trousered Philanthropists* by *Robert Tressell* and from that moment onwards it all changed.

The book is, in effect, the bible for *Christian Socialists* and one of the people on the board was John Stuart Roberts, then *Head of Television* at *BBC Wales*.

Little did I know but John was also a major supporter of Christian Socialism – and the movement has a great tradition.

I'll let *The BBC* newsreader Huw Edwards explain many years ago his background: "John won't mind me saying that he's a maverick – a Congregationalist minister who became a very talented broadcaster and executive... John was rather a scary figure: he enjoyed his (deserved) reputation as a free-thinking, provocative, unpredictable figure who openly despised the leaden ways of BBC management at that time".

93

From the moment I said what I was reading, the whole interview changed.

"Oh! Are you really?" exclaimed John.

"That's a marvellous book isn't it?".

The questions became easier and I could sense the mood of the board was warming towards me.

Needless to say, I got the job and spent 23 largely happy years at *The BBC*.

From *BBC Wales Today* I moved to Television Current Affairs and the regular series *Week In, Week Out (WIWO)*, which has now sadly been axed in favour of the occasional programme *BBC Wales Investigates*.

I covered innumerable stories and presented dozens of programmes on both television and radio, at *The BBC* based in Cardiff and London.

I hosted a live *BBC Radio* debate series which toured Wales called 'The People's Assembly', and several daily radio programmes.

Apart from WIWO, I also presented a number of *Newsnight* films and *Panorama* episodes, and I was lucky enough to win several awards.

But my different style of journalism, and long career in *The BBC*, was due, really, to a book.

No Access All Areas

As anyone who knows me will testify, I walk with a stick now. In a few years I will probably be in a wheelchair. I suffer from an incurable condition called *Hereditary Spastic Paraplegia (HSP)*.

As my consultant explained it, this is basically a corrosion of the nerves which tell your legs to do what you want them to do. In years to come only stem cell research MAY find a solution, but in the meantime, it becomes slightly worse every day. It is a rare disease, but mainly because it is often misdiagnosed as rheumatism. Sometimes there is not even a handrail on stairs, let alone a lift, and then I am completely knackered. In many ways though, I am lucky. There is no pain and a lot of people are far worse off.

The trick with any disability (and I am not saying I possess it) is NOT to compare yourself with the way you once were, because that way lies madness, but to compare yourself with other people. Then you realise that others are in far worse situations.

The main problem is that your self-image is eroded.

I used to think I was a tireless, go-getting reporter, yet now I realise I am just a disabled bloke with a stick!

I long ago stopped looking at the reflection in shop windows because of this man hobbling around who was staring back at me!

All of this was thrown into stark relief for me by David Blunkett's description of the problems he faced when he suddenly lost his guide dog Cosby. He wrote: "For the first time in my life, certainly my adult life, I felt blind. This may sound strange. Of course, I am blind. I have not been able to see throughout my entire life, although I have had perception of light and dark. But being blind and feeling blind are two very different things".

He told how he discovered walking with a long cane, the bits of buildings that he never knew existed, and how he sometimes tripped over objects that had been carelessly left unattended by their owners.

Lord Blunkett also wrote in very moving terms how all disabled people want is DIGNITY. I know exactly where he is coming from. But to dignity I would add the fact that we want to be treated exactly the same as EVERYONE ELSE.

This means that people need to think more.

The thoughtlessness of others is far worse than the education I survived, or the other illnesses I have suffered.

It may sound like this is a criticism of people, but I have always found them extremely kind and helpful when things are pointed out. The problem is they simply do not THINK about the little things that make the lives of disabled people easier. It just does not register in their consciousness for them.

For example, kerbs at key points on pavements could be lower. Those knobbly lower kerbs at corners are great, but they are not enough. We need them in the middle as well.

Paving slabs on pavements need to be more even. Usually I risk life and limb by walking in the road because the surface is much smoother.

The ramp into a public building or office is usually located far away from the direct steps to the front door, and you feel like an outcast using it.

I stress once again, that you just wish to be treated exactly the same as everybody else. Little thought for the disabled has gone into the creation of public buildings, and the number of times I have been unable to get to my seat to see something are legion.

For example, I saw a play once and my seat was at the back of the auditorium WITHOUT a handrail. The friend who was with me literally had to CARRY me to my seat, which was extremely kind of him but very undignified!

On another occasion in London I could, again, get into the auditorium of the theatre, but my seat was down a flight of stairs again without a handrail. I told the attendant there was no way I could get to my seat and I was preparing to go outside until a generous man offered me his own seat near to where I was standing stranded with my stick.

When I went to see a recent *Cardiff City v Man City* football game at the *Cardiff City Stadium,* I could drag myself up the steps into the stadium because there was a handrail, but the seat itself was up another flight of steps once more without a handrail, and then past a number of people.

There was no way I could reach it.

I went back down the steps, resigned to seeing the match on the TV screen under the stand, but in fairness the stewards came to get me and gave me a special disabled person's seat right by the touchline. It was a much better seat in fact! But the humiliating experience made me realise this whole system needs to be re-thought.

Lord Blunkett stated: "Throughout my years in government I never wanted to be the spokesman for the disabled. That would have been to undermine the raison d'être of everything I was doing — demonstrating that I could work on equal terms with anyone else".

I would never claim to be in his league, either with what he has achieved (he was after all *Home Secretary* in the early 2000s), or how he has coped with his disability. But I know exactly what he means.

You want to be 'on equal terms with anyone else' – let's hope there is change, but I doubt it somehow!

Prison Programme

As a journalist (especially an investigative one) you are often asked 'what is the story you most remember?'.

The answer is easy - an episode of the *BBC Wales TV* Current Affairs programme I presented *Week In, Week Out,* called *A Night To Remember* from 1997.

We discovered new evidence which led to the release from prison of the *Cardiff Newsagent Three* who had been wrongly convicted of murder.

Three young South Wales men, Michael O'Brien, Darren Hall and Ellis Sherwood, were out one night and had been arrested by the police later for the murder of a Cardiff newsagent and stealing his takings.

They had no reliable alibi for their correct whereabouts and unfortunately one of the three, Darren Hall, 'confessed' to the murder and also claimed that the other two were involved.

Mr. Hall said that after the newsagent was attacked, the three had run from the scene of the crime and divided up the stolen money in a nearby church yard.

A succession of prosecution witnesses in the ensuing court case 'corroborated' the confession.

When we heard of the case and started investigating it, they were at that time the longest serving jailed wrongful conviction prisoners in Wales.

We felt something was not right, and carefully looked at the evidence, found a solicitor for them and a sceptical barrister

99

who examined it all for us.

I interviewed Mr Hall in prison, permission for which is rarely given now, and asked him directly: *"Did you do the murder?".*

"No, I didn't and nor did the other two", came the reply.

Phil interviewed Darren Hall in prison who said he did not do it. © BBC

I talked to, and recorded, over the telephone, Mr O'Brien who said a terrible injustice had been done, both to them and the loved ones of the murdered newsagent.

We filmed Mr O'Brien's family in the Ely area of Cardiff, whose lives, needless to say, had been devastated.

We tracked down all the 'witnesses' who were, to a lesser or greater extent, unreliable.

We discovered that Mr Hall during or after one of his interviews, he claimed, had been manacled to a radiator.

Crucially, we found new medical evidence in records that proved Mr Hall's story could never have happened.

His legs were bad and he could not have joined the others in running away from the scene of the murder to divide up the spoils, as had been claimed.

The original court case was totally flawed.

I pay tribute in this to my producer at the time, who went on to edit the series, *Karen Voisey,* who assembled much of the evidence, and to the Editor of *Week In, Week Out,* Adrian Davies, who commissioned the programme and continued in his confidence of us, even though one of the lawyers rang him at home to say there was not enough evidence.

There were, of course, many very dark moments.

I clearly remember taking Karen for a chat on a bench outside the BBC after one of them and telling her we should stick with it, because we were right.

The three men were ultimately released after 11 years in jail, and I felt it had been a job well done.

Phil presented new evidence on Current Affairs TV which led to the release from prison of Ellis Sherwood, Darren Hall and Michael O'Brien after a wrongful conviction for murder. ©BBC

It is nice to think that occasionally journalism can do some good...

9 781916 453296